# Nascent Wings

# Nascent Wings

## A POETIC ENDEAVOR

## SURABHI

PARTRIDGE
A Penguin Company

**Partridge books may be ordered through booksellers or by contacting:**

Partridge India
Penguin Books India Pvt. Ltd
11, Community Centre, Panchsheel Park, New Delhi 110017
India
www.partridgepublishing.com
Phone: 000.800.10062.62

# Contents

## ❖ *SOCIETY*

## ❖ *LOVE*

## ❖ *CHANGE*

*"The birth of an idea in the mind is worthy, only when, it is conceived by the heart and reproduced in deeds."*

*Surabhi*

To Grand pa (Papa), my inspiration and my ideal

For Daddy, my best friend and 'unconditional' supporter

# *Acknowledgement*

I pay humble and sincere thanks to my entire family for their support. I also thank God for his blessings.

I am thankful to my grandparents for their blessings in my endeavours, my mother for always inspiring me to give my hundred percent in whatever I do by being my biggest critic, my brother and sister-in-law for their unconditional love showered at me non-stop, and not to forget, my friends for always being there.

I pay my heartfelt gratitude to my father for his unconditional support and faith in me. His encouragement and unshakable trust have always been the wings to my dreams. Love you, Daddy.

I am thankful to James Clifford, Ann Minoza and the rest of the team at Partridge for their patience and support at every level of the book's publication.

I thank Mr. Uma Shankar for the perfect illustrations at such short notice.

I owe all my skills to my teachers, especially, Mr. Amber Bannerjee and other teachers at BR DAV Public School, IOC, Bihar and Mr. Anandi Shankar Singh (my English tuition teacher). I pay my sincere thanks to them.

Last but definitely not the least, I would like to thank the entire faculty of my college Pran's Media, Noida for brushing up my skills and providing me numerous opportunities to improve and excel.

I am thankful to everyone who encouraged me and stood by my side.

# Introduction

'**Nascent Wings**'—*A poetic endeavor* is basically a collection of poems categorised under distinct themes. The poems were written randomly with no intentions of any thematic categorisation initially. Later on, I observed that all my poems could easily be classified under certain genres or topics.

This categorisation not only highlights the mood of the poems but it also makes the poetic journey of the reader methodical. As per mood, a particular poem can be easily selected to read. This also felicitates the idea of relating to the particular mood as per the reader's choice.

Poetry is a very interesting form of literature. It evokes symbolic meanings. '**Nascent Wings**' *A poetic endeavor* is a humble attempt at meaningful poetry. This is my debut book.

I have made an attempt to reach the hearts of the readers, share my views and ideas on various relative topics through '**Nascent Wings**' *A poetic endeavor*.

From social issues to emotional strains, from motivation to the madness of love, it is a holistic poetic journey that offers vivid flavours to the readers.

Happy reading!

Surabhi

# 'Motivation'

This set of poems is very positive and encouraging.

Readers can enjoy reading any of the poems under this section anytime, to get a moral upliftment and boost.

As the name of the theme clearly suggests, this set of poems is motivating and inspirational.

The poems in this section promote the idea of taking steps towards your goals and not getting disappointed by failures. Life is all about learning and moving ahead.

# Nascent Wings

I feel an instant urge,
To fly and to submerge,

Above the sky, and into the sea,
Pave my own golden destiny

"God helps them, who help themselves"
Everyone around since childhood yells

Today, at 20 I realise
It's not just a saying, rather an advice

To let out the fears & take a leap
For my own dreams, I need to speak

Not only through words, rather deeds
For success needs labour and heed

The hunger to accomplish & achieve
Will increase the urge to succeed

I will bloom with nascent wings
I will bloom with nascent wings

## "To know what you want"

When I was a kid,
I wanted to be a doctor
Not that I knew what it meant
It was what I was told to be

When I was in my early teens
I dreamt to be a dancer
Not that I was aware
Of the mind-set of people around me

When I passed matriculation
I aspired to be a writer
Not that I was influenced
That was exactly what I could ever be

I tried and tried and I am
Still trying
Not that I am not happy
But, "perfection" is what I seek

To know what you want is good enough
Not that "perfection" is an easy stuff
"Keep trying, never quit"
Is the slogan to succeed!

# Life

Life is the ultimate chance
To remain joyous or to have a grievance

It is the start and end of all
It's someone's rise and someone's fall

I have had an eventful life
Joy, dismay, excitement, pride

Have experienced various emotions
Done things, good, and worth corrections

Haven't seen God but have seen parents
Showering forgiveness and endurance

I have a sweet enduring bro
He is a true gem that I know

Grandparents and rest family
Are jubilant and supportive equally

I realise I have cursed
Life, with mistakes that can't be reversed

My follies have caused them pain
I know I've acted imprudent, insane

I am lucky to have mum-dad
They show me hope and make me glad

They brighten my life like emerald
Life is beautiful again, a herald

Of hope dream and joyous fragrance
I am stunned by calm endurance

Life is really the biggest teacher
'To learn' is man's best feature

Live Life with **positive vision**
Easily accomplished, will be every mission!

## *At times . . .*

At times I feel I hate me
At times, I hate time gloomy
At times I feel no it's okay
Everyone learns from dismay

At times, I feel I am lucky
At times it seems I'm unlucky
At times I feel no it's fine
All is controlled by power divine

At times I feel I should die
At times I feel I should survive
At times I feel one day will come
When all will be easy, positive and fun

At times I feel I am a shame
To my parents, I give a lot of pain
At times I feel it is the rule
Man learns from faults, who doesn't is a fool!!

At times I feel it's always better
To be a hard working Trier
At times I feel stop sulking!
Dream and work towards achieving!

Why do we fall, remember forever
So that we can get up; **never say never**!!

# The time to pray

The time to pray is not when in crisis,
But, as soon as you are out of it
God allows all in his divine premises,
In devotion, the ray of hope is always lit

Whenever you are in despair,
Cobwebbed with worldly cares
Be honest and work real hard
Have faith in the Lord

He will lead you to the right,
Path and he will help you fight
All the dark phases of life
Free you of the negative strife

Just at the moment you survive out
Grateful prayers should involuntarily sprout
Towards the Lord for benediction
That gave you strength and conviction

To keep trying with faith and trust
And kept away morbid self-disgust

Don't pray when it rains
If you don't pray when the sun shines
Only honest prayers gain
The bliss of the divine

# By yourself

Teachers open the door,
You enter by yourself
If you want to achieve something
Then stir the life of shelf!

Teachers, guides and mentors
Can enlighten you about the path
But the efforts will be yours
And yours will be the wrath

To accomplish, you have to decide
You have to work and you have to stride
Only **by yourself**, you can gain
True efforts never go in vain

Sitting idle complaining
"I don't have the right teacher"
That is mere guilt in feign
And not an endeavour

God helps them who try and labour
Laziness, lethargy, God never favours
Life is short, it is your take
To be a star, or a soul—nonchalant and opaque

# *The art of being wise*

The art of being wise,
Sage and sapient
Actually lies
In a very non-lenient
Idea of knowing, what to overlook
What to permit and what not to brook

Apply the phrase "ignorance is bliss"
Wherever required this saying assists
To avoid unnecessary cobwebs of tension
Cure is good, the best is prevention

The best aid to focus
Is selective permeability
Overlook the trivial
And avoid negativity

Atrocious elements have abominable influence
They divert our energy and lead to abhorrence
So the art of being wise is in the clear detection
Of what to focus on, what's not worth selection?

Be wise and overlook to focus on the paramount
Consistent and steady labour facilitates your surmount.

# *Stand*

Those who stand for nothing fall for anything
They are vulnerable, at whatever, they fling
They don't bear any specific identity
They die ordinary, behold no amenity

Stand for a cause believe in a purpose
Live on principles work with focus
Man is an animal distinct from the rest
His benedictions are brain and quest

A life of goals and ambitions
Drives life to a worthy destination
To err, to learn, to fall and stand
To endure, move ahead and withstand

Are essential for progress
For a meaningful life and success

Those who stand for nothing fall for anything
They are dubious, at whatever, they sling
Before it starts, they lose the race
They are inane, a transparent face . . .

# The opposite of love

The opposite of love is not hate
Hatred is an emotion that abates
Positive energy into exasperation
It deviates us from our destination

The opposite of love is indifference
Not imprudent detest or abhorrence
Odium instigates a regressive nature
It is of no utility, curbs your future

If someone does not deserve you love
Don't love him, it's fair enough
Investing an emotion as strong as hate
Is absolutely wrong, why spoil your fate?

Indifferent attitude is the best key
To apply in this case, oh! Trust me
Remember what Bapu defined
An eye for an eye would make the world blind!

Be calm, composed and concentrate on
Peace and progress, you were not born
To spread the message of retribution
Or to practise abomination

The opposite of love is not hate,
Rather, apathetical indifference.

# What you do

People may doubt what you say
But they will always believe what you do

Believe in acting more than you utter
Hollow words may make you stutter
If tomorrow you somehow fail
People's doubt will never grant you a bail

People may doubt what you say
But they will always believe what you do

Perform your plans with dedication
Achieve your goals to win elation
Don't give the society a chance
With deeds you can enhance
Your tract of trust and notability
Drive away the ambiguity

People may doubt what you say
But they will always believe what you do
More than words, performance weighs
No one can deny as this is true!

# *Reality of 'roots'*

People who remember where they are from
People who never forget, to where they belong
People who are aware of the reality of 'roots'
Have an unshakable foundation, they never lose

Whatever heights you attain in life
Always remember, to avoid strife
Remain solid on your basic principle
Those who forget, face consequences, fatal

They either deviate from their moral values
Or end up with hollow views
Such people tend to be hypocrites
Living in double standards and painful plights

Your roots remind you of the basic culture
An instinct to build an honest future
With lessons taught by mother and life
With success and joy forever you thrive

Remembering reality of 'roots' is right
Reasonable enough as it invites
True happiness and turns you into
A good human being, honest and true

Whatever you achieve, wherever you go
You must deep down always know
Who are you? Where are you from?
Who are you? Where are you from?

# '*Pangs of pain*'

'*Pangs of pain*' is a set of emotional poems that narrates feelings of loneliness, broken heart and nostalgia.

This set of poems has a collection of, basically, sad poesy that take you to the journey of strong emotions like nostalgia and deplorable separation from loved ones.

This set of poems is very emotionally engrossing and a sentimental tryst. I am sure the verses will agitate and unsheathe vivid emotions of the readers.

# Darkest Night

I look out my window
Into the black of night
My body quivers
Full of a curious fright

I turn away
And crawl back in bed
The air is musty
The world is dead

Tossing and turning
I try and relax
It's like stepping
On millions of tacks

Again, I rise and pace the floor
My body aches my heart is sore
Why is it that I now want to cry?
Life is better but I still want to die

These emotions are overcoming my soul
I am falling down
Into the darkest hole

Oh! Where is my love
When I need him so
He is the one who can make
My happiness show

With his arms around me
I feel delight
I don't have to worry
I don't need to fight

I look out my window
Into the light of day
My words become lost
I have nothing to say

# "It makes me feel hollow"

Sometimes the best paroles
Make you feel hollow
The love that enlivens you
Also gives sorrow . . .

I don't understand how to satisfy
How to make him happy and how to clarify
That everything I do, is for him
From my huge decisions to a tiny sniff!

Why can't he just let me be?
Accept me the way I am "ME"

I love him, his plus his minuses
Just because he embraces
Me, with love, care and concern
Then why does he want me to discern

Myself into:
"A version of his"
When I want to enjoy the bliss

Of being me and still being loved
Not being altered or submerged
Into a sea of self-derision
This will kill the pious passion . . .

A perfect person is scarce to find
Loving is in acceptance defined!!

Sometimes the best paroles
Make you feel hollow
The love that enlivens you
Also gives sorrow . . .

# Life Goes On!

You came into my life
As soul mates we thrived

Your embrace touched my soul
'You and I' was my goal

I loved you, you loved me back
I felt my life had no lack
We cherished our love divine
Everything was perfectly fine

Alas! Came a catastrophic storm!
Life was in pieces torn!
You said, "Love, It didn't work"
Hah! My fate, what a jerk!

You left me to suffer, solitary
I tried by frown and by plea
To stop you, but all in vain
You left, you never came back again!

Till date my eyes are waiting
Desperate, love thirsty, not letting
Me to live, or love or 'move-on'
But as they, "life goes on" . . .
It does go on!
It does go on!

# Solitary

Today I am a solitary soul
In this world, completely alone

There's no one who understands
My complicated and simple strands

No one who says, 'keep going'
No warm embraces no consoling

I am forced to think it hard
What wrong emotion did I impart?

To end up like a lonely star
Visible alone like a scar

In the darkest nights of all
Petrified, worried, scared to fall

There is only single ray
Of hope, that would drive away

Weariness and my entire fears
And help me rise above my peers

Self-confidence and hard work
In consistence have a huge perk

One day I will rise above
And the world will shower love . . .

But, Today I am a solitary soul
In this world, completely alone

There's no one who understands
My complicated and simple strands . . .

# "Though the friend slays you"

Gone are those days of amazing fun
When we were a pair of bonded chums
Just like orange juice and rum
Together at night and in the sun . . .

You were a friend who was like a sister
Until that event happened, it was sinister!

He came into your life; robbed me of my mate
Not that I wasn't happy for you, but fate
Had secret plans, I wish you had paid
A slight heed to whatever I had said . . .

You were so smitten, I was afraid
You'd chose him, despite of my warnings, instead
You did exactly what my guts had warned
I was petrified and you were lost in charm

You could not see his devil intentions
He was a scoundrel and he hurt your emotions

He robbed your money and your soul
And then he dragged you into a hole

Of torture, pain and repeated assault
And then you said it was my fault!

You accused me of not being worthy
Of love of friendship or mercy
I am imprisoned for conspiracy
I wonder where the true culprit is . . .

My mistake was that I had gone to meet
And called him a few times in a week

But it was to warn him to give me back
My friend, my sister, but there was lack
Of trust for me in your heart!
To my surprise, you threw us apart . . .

I am imprisoned for conspiracy
I wonder where the true culprit is . . .

Gone are those days of amazing fun
When we were a pair of bonded chums
Just like orange juice and rum
Together at night and in the sun . . .

## "When you dismiss yourself to love"

You turn calm like a dove
When you dismiss yourself to love

He does all that he wants to do
Things that might even hurt you

You see, you feel but still can not
Absorb the fact of distraught!

You feel upset and agitated
He cares the least, you are irritated

It seems like an unsolved puzzle
Chaotic, bothering like a hassle!

He loves, he cares, and he endures you
But still at times, he injures you

With his attraction for worldly affairs
His lies, his circle—all hidden shares!!

You turn meek and submissive
When you dismiss yourself to love

Is it a curse or is it bliss?
When you dismiss yourself to love . . .

# Let another eon pass by

Let another eon pass by
I am not ready to make a try
For myself or my life
I've become accustomed to this wry

He mauled my heart with cavalier
Our relationship was a failure
May be I was not good enough
I could not detect the ongoing bluff

He slaughtered my heart and went away
He tattered my dreams in such a way
My soul shivers even today
He abandoned me, he betrayed

My love my being my existence
I think I have lost the tolerance
I can't let go, I can't move on
I am lost astray since an eon

Let another eon pass by
Tears have fogged the sight of eyes
The wound is new, life is dismal
There is no hue, I feel abysmal

Let another eon pass by
It's hard to live, it's harder to die
Let another eon pass by

# *Infidelity*

Infidelity is not covert
Infidelity is so overt
Needs no skills to subvert
Infidelity is morally corrupt

It is clear and very apparent
Can't be hidden for long, it is declarant
Immediately perceived and understood
To be overlooked, it is too aberrant

Words are not needed to remove the veil
The awkward behaviour, the indifferent feel
Does the imparting; the lies, the ignorance,
And the fear of being revealed

Infidelity not only slays
The heart of the lover, it also betrays
Foundations of trust and pious faith

Unfaithfulness and Infidelity impart
Pangs of pain and separation
Peace from life forever departs
Leaving behind exasperation

It is a sin, a salvation,
Reaches to no destination
Be honest when in love
Remember one day fate will delve

Infidelity is a soul slayer
I can say as I've met a betrayer
Who ruined my emotions and left me astray
I knew he was a bluffer, long before he said
That he had found another mate
May no one encounter such afflicting fate!

Infidelity is not covert
Infidelity is so overt
Needs no skills to subvert
Infidelity is morally corrupt

# Rueful 'ME'

Regret is like a termite
It makes you hollow from inside

Once smitten by remorse
It is not easy to change that course . . .
. . . Of undergoing self pity
It shakes your emotional entity

Anger, sorrow and contrite
Ruthful feeling is a plight

I can't help I am stuck
I regret, I curse my luck
For a mistake unforgivable,
A blunder so abominable

I broke his heart and disappeared
From his life within mere
Nascent days of love and trust
I know it was unfair, not just

Though, I had my reasons to
Do what I did, this is true

Still I cannot till today
Recover the guilt or drive away
The pity and self abhorrence
I am in a rueful existence

How I wish I could somehow
Let him know and clear his doubt

"I never wished to lose you mate"
I think you were not in my fate

What I did was a helpless cry
To settle something, but I don't deny
It gave you a lot of pain
And my life has become a rueful vain

# *I wish I had no heart*

I wish I had no heart, no feelings, and no emotions
Life would be only about logic and rationalisation

I wish I had no heart, no love and no sorrow
No sentiments to lend to the world, no sentiments to borrow

I wish I had no heart, no trust and no betrayal
No love to give, no faith to keep and no secrets to share

I wish I had no heart, no butterflies at his sight
No goose bumps, no passion and no separation plight

I wish I had no heart, no kindness no generosity
Only give and take, no considerations and no charity

Wait a minute! But, would life be, as beautiful, as now?
Despite of the pains and cruelties of the world, I don't know,
somehow
I suddenly feel the urge to stop making this wish
Because without the heart there will be a lot that I will miss

Sorrow and joy, love and grief, emotions passion and feel
These are significant colours of life that make it worth living

I wish I had never met that heart that led to my moral fall
I wish to have a stronger heart, rather than no heart at all!!

# '*Society*'

In this segment of 'Nascent Wings', I have made an attempt to cover relevant issues of the social system of our nation.

This set of poems is neither a 'complaint section' nor an 'appraisal wing' of the society; rather it talks about mixed issues, covering the positive aspects as well as the negative ones expressed in rhythmic verses.

This section is an amazing combination of poetry on a spectrum of social issues, i.e. negative to neutral to positive.

47

## "Not a Miss"

I am an embryo
My father wants to kill me
My fault, I don't know
I think because I am a 'She' . . .

I am an infant
Thrown into a drainage
What harm could I
Possibly do, at my tender age?

I am a baby girl
Tortured by my teacher
Bad things he does to me
No one is my believer!

I am a teenager
The world seems like a hawk
Someone stares at my front
Someone pinches my back!!

I am a college girl
Molested, raped and thrown
They say that there must've been
Something wrong that I had worn!!

I am a woman
Married to a devil
Drunkard, chauvinist, torturer
To the extent of peril!

I am an educated lady
Independent and smart
They say the reason to success
Is surely being "character-dwarf"!!

I am an old lady
Mauled by my son
He beats me up for money
Sometimes for mere fun!

Today I am relieved
From the pain of life
I am a corpse, a happy one
I induced death with a knife . . .

I am a soul in heaven
God asks me what I wish
I say, Dear God! Make me anything,
Even worm, but NOT A "MISS"!!

# We love India—Gen XYZ!

India, India, We love you
In our colleges, in our schools

Every day we pray for your
Development and progress more!

We are the media, we the politics
We the players, we do the remix

We are dying on L.O.C.
"Developed India"-we foresee!

They say we are not devoted
But, we are so motivated

For our country for our land
Our patriotism is very grand . . .

India, India, We love you
In our colleges, in our schools

Every day we pray for your
Development and progress more!

## "Journey"

Journey gives experience
Journey is an experiment, Journey shows places
Helps us meet faces

Journey is an adventure, Journey is fascination
Sometimes it is fun
Sometimes a depression!

Journey is essential,
To see the world around
It felicitates the 'commercial'
As few professions are bound

Journey teaches variety, it is a guarantee
For fun, for frolic, for joy
Keep travelling my boy!

Journey gives education
Journey is an endeavour, Journey shows places
Helps us meet faces . . .

# "An air of disdain"

I am ninety and obviously old
Fragile, weak and not so bold

Physical meekness is not what hurts
It is acceptable and natural course

That what eats me from within . . .
Is, the termite of loathing

From those kids whom I bore
In my womb; I endured

Their failures and success
But today I'm just a mess

A burden, a pathetic member
Who ruins their parties or slumber!

Whenever they visit me here
In my home, "old age sphere"

I always feel an air of disdain
And that gives me excruciating pain

All I pray to power divine
My kids don't get kids like mine!!

# Paying silver paying gold;
# Poverty, literacy and the old?

Paying silver paying gold;
Poverty, literacy and the old-
Are major troubles so ignored!
Superstitions, Corruption, Fraud

Being enhanced by this dodge
"Rich-elite" wake-up now
Stop being social blows, somehow,

Do charity for the weak
Temple donations are so bleak!

Rich getting richer and poor-poorer
Renovation in society should start sooner

Stop being blind, use your mind
Better reasons to spend, you will find!!

Paying silver paying gold;
Poverty, literacy and the old-
Are major troubles so ignored!

# "India hai toh line toh hogi hi!"

Yeh India hai meri jaan!
Apna pyara Hindustan . . .

Any work here is due
If you've not been part of a queue!

Ticket-counters to showroom entries
Public toilets, anywhere in the country
Witness lines of impatient masses
Fight starts if anyone surpasses!

Only the elite people are privileged
To get their jobs done without lines
The common man suffers, he is frustrated
And later on they say—Chalo, its fine!

"Bade logon k kaam aise hi hote hain,
Hamein to chappal ghisna hai, sikke hi khote hain!!"

Hostility, unawareness and corruption
Lead to the "line me ao" wali frustration
"Line lagi hai bhai, andhe ho kya"?
"4 dino se khada hun, tum Birla k bande ho kya?"

Auditions, interviews, form submissions,
Ye India hai bhai,
Queues are a compulsion!

# *"Hue is for life"*

What would be the world like?
If there were no colours
May be like plain ice-creams
Without any flavours

Colours enrich the world with
Visual appeal
Symbols, meanings, vividness-
So much they conceal

Take 'red', its love, danger and hot
'Green' is soothing, white is peace
'Black' may be what is not!

Colours behold true magic
Love, success or tragic
Every emotion carries its hue
Yellow, orange, grey or blue!

Without colours the world would seem
Bleached of all the livelihood
Rainbows, fashion, Science, Nature
Paintings, people, Bollywood!!

What would be the world like?
If there were no colours
May be like plain ice-creams
Without any flavours

# Accountability

To allege the government for all the woes
In the nation, and to accuse
The system for every lack
Is an easy task, for citizens who are slack

But it is time to realise,
To take serious responsibility
Contribute your part, be prudent and wise
Play your role, commit to liability

You litter the roads, don't step out to vote
You leave the tap running, don't switch off the light
Do you feel guilty at this note?
Citizens' ignorance is India's biggest plight

It is high time, wake up India
Taking accountability is a fabulous idea
Perform your duties and get your rights
That will be a fair fight

Corruption is not a single dimension
It prevails at every level
Passport, D.L. whatever documentation
To us, **bribing**, seems to be an easier vehicle

So, first be self analytical
Rectify your deeds then be critical
To the system or authority
Wake up India! Take accountability

# Save life on earth

Save trees save life on earth
There is an extreme dearth
Of greenery and, ecological
Turbulence, is very critical

Dolphins, elephants, leopards, sparrows
Tigers, turtles, gorillas and rhinos
Many more species to enlist
Are on the verge of getting extinct

Global warming has alarming effects
Endangered species to climate change facets
About 3.3 mm per year
Rise in sea level is another fear

Plant more trees, promote plantation
Avoid unnecessary air pollution
Keep a check on CO2,
By burning less fossil fuel

Either walk or ride a cycle
To the nearby places
'Save the environment' sing this recital
To save lives of species

This is an urgent mission
No more, it can be ignored
Love Mother Earth, to love your lives
Work together in galore

Not as a state, not as a nation
Neither as a continent
This problem has to be addressed
Like a 'Planet' in union

# *Culturally rich*

An amalgamation of several cultures,
With traditions that are centuries old
Indian cuisine, yoga and religions
Have profound impact across the globe

One of the most religiously diverse nations,
India is the birth place of various religions
Various languages and hundreds of dialects
'Unity in diversity' describes India the best

Kathakalli, Kuchipudi Bihu, Bharatnatyam
Odissi, Sattriya, Mohiniyattam
Garba, Ghoomar, Bhangra and Giddha
Are few to name dance forms of mother India

Vedas, Puranas and the Shastras
Enrich the mythology while Sanskrit shlokas
Are chanted for eternal peace
By common people and Hindu priests

Aryabhatta, Chanakya, Homi Bhabha
Sushruta, bhaskara, Charaka, Vyasa
Are world known scientists of our nation
Significant, eminent are their contributions

Rajasthan is rich with Flawless forts
Rich heritage of India surely imports
Tourists from all over the world
Royal culture India beholds

Geographically, the seventh largest
Biggest democracy on the planet
Himalayas as crown in the North
The South is completely ocean bound

An amalgamation of several cultures,
With traditions that are centuries old

# The Dark Visage

I lived in a cave for a long time
It was warm and safe
I liked it there, it was cosy
My home, my lovely cave

I was happily growing
Until one day, I felt
Excess movement, expulsion
Almost like a swing

I was forced to escape out,
Through a very narrow tunnel
I wept, I was afraid
At the sudden newness

There was light, I could not see
But I heard voices in vicinity
One voice said, 'it would've been easier with safety'
Another voice, a familiar one
Replied in a choked tone
'This is not a great time; lecture me once this trouble is gone'

Before I could realise,
I was trashed into something
I could not open my eyes
I heard the word 'Polythene'

I think after a little while I felt I was in air
I was crying loud suffocated wondering why was I here?
Another instant I felt a thud
My head hit something hard
Next thing I know I lay in mud
With rotten legs and body scarred

I had been half eaten by some deadly animal
What was left of me was rotten and detestable

Suddenly the air had a strange ferocity
Fear drenched me as I looked with curiosity
A big animal, 4 legged, with sharp teeth
Approached me and it seeped
My flesh with its fangs
Excruciating pain took away my life with a bang!!

Today I am a melancholy soul
Betrayed by the birth-giver
Can a mother be this cruel?
Even at the thought, I shiver . . .

# *'Love'*

Obviously, this section of the collection is all about love, desire and passion. This set of poems can be very easily related to.

All of us fall in love or dream of what would falling in love be like. I have tried to conceal my ideas of love and fantasy into poetry and presented here.

This section of 'Nascent wings' sings the melody of mad, silly, imprudent love.

It talks about intense passion and pure dedication. It enchants the beauty of selflessness and romance.

# Soul Survives For Thee

You inspire life into me
My soul survives for thee
You are that priceless asset
That makes my life perfect

You are an admirable gem
You make me crazy and insane
Cannot imagine a second without you
Dear soul mate, I love you!

You are the best part of life
For you I shall always strive
You complete my half existence
I pray "us" to be in consistence

You are so cute, I adore you
You are so simple, am flattered by you
You are a unique creation of God
At times I feel, are you real or not!

You have a pious divine essence
I am bestowed with your presence
You truly inspire life into me
My soul survives only for thee.

# "In that glance, two eyes became four"

In that glance, two eyes became four
Suddenly life seemed to be much more
Than books or food or music or sleep
Through eyes, into my soul he seeped

My world took a drastic turn
The glance of his eyes was so stern
Holding my feet was not gravity
He became the very central potency

I became aware of every cell,
Of my body like never before
His eyes, his aura and his smell
Overwhelmed my every pore!!

Love flooded my veins and heart
That glance marked a brand new start
I discovered, within me, an inner Goddess
Dancing, frolicking in madness

Logic, Quant, Rationalisation
Were replaced with fascination
In that glance, two eyes became four
Suddenly life seemed to be much more . . .

# LOVE

Love is ecstasy
Love is fantasy

Love cures all pain
Love, till end, remains

Love is an element for all relations
It strengthens bonds, enriches emotions

Love is life and life is small
So give love to one and all

Mother, father, friends and foes
Love to all one must bestow

Spread love and get it back
Wt's life, if in love, it lacks

Love is ecstasy
Love is fantasy

Love cures all pain
Love, till end, remains . . .

# Cupid

Cupid is the God of love and affection
Son of the Love Goddess Venus,
Representative of attraction

Depiction of a naked winged child, typically with a bow
Cupid injects love, into his victims, using his arrow

Symbol of love, erotic and intense
Spreads fondness by mere presence

Cupid is an icon of passion and amative
Infects spoilt love like a purgative

Cupid inspires fidelity
Emotions of love and honesty
Cupid spreads pious amour
Into the game of heart, he lures

Cupid is the God of love and affection
Son of the Love Goddess Venus, representative of attraction
All of us definitely, get, one day, smitten
By Cupid's beautiful and lovely infection!

# Valentine's Day

The feast of Saint Valentine,
As the 'day of love' is defined
Observed on February 14 each year
To propagate love and to adhere

To peace, fondness and compassion
Valentine's Day is the day of affection

Lovers, children, families
Come together in amative

Red roses and soft hearts
People exchange beautiful cards

The feast of Saint Valentine,
Is celebrated in the world to remind
The significance of the idea of love
Compassion for people and God above . . .

# Beyond my control

We met after a decade,
All by chance, by mere fate

There was something that took me by surprise
The electricity in the air
The same awkwardness, it was a reprise
Of the pure love we shared

The first time we met, we were hardly ten
Didn't know what love or attraction meant

Still, there was a new effervescent
Froth of butterflies for each other
You liked me and I liked you
In the 5 days school camp, that together we spent

After the school camp was over
You and I saw each other never
Until in November last year
Fate brought us together and near

There was an air of love and passion
With time we had grown and so had our compassion

I had an image of the kid I loved
For a decade that I savoured
But, other than the shock of that intense feeling
There was another thing equally amazing

Your hazel eyes, your broad shoulders
The hint of stubble slight beard
Your tall structure and beautiful face
My heartbeats took a different pace

Your sight was a literal visual treat
I was awe struck by your appeal

We stared at each other for a while
I felt so smitten in the prime
Of my youth, to love palpable
In that instant I was unable
To say anything or justify
I was in deep love, mystified

They say first love never fails
Am sure this is a true hail
I have felt it in my life
I have my love as my life . . .

I am deeply in love with you
You are my life and its hue . . .
There is an air of love and passion
With you as a partner, life has new dimensions!

# The way I love you

I was, not a bit, aware
I could love the way I love you
The emotion that I share
With you is so pious and so true

Your eyes, your smile, your cute pranks on me
Your angelic voice, your incredible ability
To make me do whatever you want
Not by force or demand
Simply because that makes me cheerful
To see a smile on your face so beautiful

Your love has an angelic touch
Sometimes I wonder, is it too much?
To be engrossed limitlessly
To be in love so deeply

Then my heart stops my mind
Saying 'love can never be defined',
Measured by quantity or in figures
All logic fails when love is triggered

You care, you share and you make love
You promise that you will never give up
On the idea of 'Me & U'
I see in your eyes that your love is true

You also seem equally smitten
By my love your life is driven
So let us keep spoiling each other's heart
With limitless love, till death do us apart

# The way you love me

The way you forget the world, when you look into my eyes
The way you cherish the moments, whenever you make me smile
The way you unconditionally support me in every way
The way you are always there, by my side you stay

The way your eyes penetrate into mine, with intense love and passion
The way you say my name, with dedicated divine devotion

The way you are always ready to do anything for me
The way you take care of everything I need

The way you respect me and my individual life
The way you blindly trust me, increases my drive
To melt in love with you forever,
And marry you to be your wife

I know I can never reciprocate the love that you shower
You are the most amazing person, you never hover
I lose patience and temper at times
But, you never get irritated
I wonder if I could be like that, always calm, never agitated!!

You have such a lovely heart and a Godly soul
What good did I ever do to be your mate, at all??
The way you say I love you, takes my breath away
I am so lucky to have you with me, to thank God I always
pray

# '*Change*'

Change is an inevitable and significant part of our lives. Some changes are positive while some are fatal. Some changes are deliberate and some consequential.

This set of poems is related to different facets of this phenomenon called '*change*'.

Poems under this section are inspirational, philosophical or simply factual.

# Be the change

'You must be the change,
You wish to see in the world
Rather than complaining
Take charge and be stern

To change what you get, change what you give
Your actions cultivate the scene in what you live
You always reap what you sow
The world will give back what you show

If you want respect, be respectful first
Change yourself and quench your thirst
Of changing the world in a positive way
If all of us act like this, the world may

Become a better place to live
Always remember, you get what you give

Rather than being a fusser and whiner
About the troubles prevailing around
Be the 'revolution' major or minor
Together we can bring changes profound

'You must be the change,
You wish to see in the world'
Follow Bapu's valuable words!

# All change is not growth

All change is not growth
As all movement is not advancement
Remember this solemn oath
All change is not a development

Don't be charmed with negative elements,
For self interest and success
Certain steps lead to regress
Before changing, analyse and assess

Think twice before you leap
Certain changes invite grief

Good and bad both prevail
Around us, and we can fail

If we do not understand
Very easily we could land
In problems and hindrances
Under negative influences

All change is not growth
As all movement is not advancement
Remember this solemn oath
All change is not a development

# Bollywood:
# 100 years of change

The journey from silent films to Dolby sound
From black and white to 3D and HD, is profound

1913 saw the first release
'Raja Harishchandra' was the movie
3<sup>rd</sup> May was the fortunate date
The film industry took birth, by fate

Bollywood is a century old
Its basic essence of vividness, it beholds
Father of Indian Cine, Sir Dada Saheb Phalke
Would be so proud today

Casting, filming, editing, songs
Every facet has undergone
Vast changes for the good
Of the films and Bollywood

Advertisements, Dialogues, Scripts and shows
International acclaim and exposure
No element has stagnated
With time our films have accepted
The change, the progress, the advancement
This is the reason of the development

As Bollywood has not grown only by age
Also in style and in technological grace
Indian cinema has the maximum
Output of films per annum

The journey from silent films to Dolby sound
From black and white to 3D and HD, is profound

# Advancement or distortion: Change happens to all

Change is not likely, it is inevitable
It either gives you stability or makes you stumble
Advancement or distortion, change happens to all
Depending on the situation, it brings rise or fall

Some changes are catastrophic
Bring despair, are enigmatic
They have to be dealt with patience and faith
**Such changes call for an immediate change**

Some changes are a life-time chance
To adapt, inculcate and advance
They have to be dealt with sincere care
You have to accept the change, you have to adhere

But, this is a fact that cannot be denied
Change happens to all, we have to abide
By all the alterations that occur to us
Changes could be small or enormous

We have to realise, we have to endure
Because they are inevitable, this is sure
Change is not likely, it is inevitable
It either gives you stability or makes you stumble

# Moral Upgradation : Call of time

"Another 5 year old raped by neighbour"
"Rape victim dies of tremor"
These are regular headlines
Biggest shame of the time

A tight slap on the face of our nation
Where ladies were regarded with devotion
The country of Goddesses
Is in a pathetic mess

Cases of rape and sexual assault, domestic violence and brutal
acts
Are no more NEWS, but everyday facts
Followed by revolts and protests
But is this the solution? Let me assess

No is the answer according to me
Being a girl I personally feel
The anger, the revolts and the fight
Is at its place, well-justified

To bring about an ACTUAL CHANGE
Every man must be trained
With moral values and education
Of treating women as <u>Homo</u> <u>sapiens</u>

Pieces of glass, bottles and iron rods, are inserted in a female's
body!!
Is this where we are going? Shouldn't this be dealt with
priority??
Not the government, not the police, no one can stop this
calamity
Until and unless, we as citizens take charge and check our
morality

The police and other authorities can take action to punish
It is us with whose efforts this disgrace can completely vanish

The ongoing scenario is no more a political issue
It is completely societal, about what the society can do
Neither the rapists nor the officials are outsiders or aliens
These people are also a part of our society, few out of the
millions

**Moral up gradation** is the call of time, to save our society
It is time for us to act; mankind is in a state of pity
He has to wake up, he has forgotten, that he is not meant
To do what he is doing, from other animals, he is different

He is a father who cares unconditionally to protect his
innocent daughter
He is a brother, an iron man, a support to his sister
He is a husband who loves his wife and is a provider
Of trust, comfort, respect and care
He is not a predator!!

**Moral up gradation** is the call of time, to save our society
It is time for us to act; mankind is in a state of pity . . .
Mankind is in a state of pity!!

# About the author

Surabhi is a final year mass communication student at Pran's Media Institute, Noida. She has been brought up in a small district called Begusarai in Bihar.

Her grandfather Dr. Sridhar Narayan Pandey is also an author and her true inspiration.

Her inclination towards writing and oratory dates back to her school days. She has been certified the 'Best Communication Skills' award by Mr. Pran Kumar Sharma, the "Walt Disney of India" and creator of "Chacha Chaudhary" at Pran's Media Institute in the year 2011.

Her hobbies are reading, writing and dancing. 'Nascent Wings'—A poetic endeavour is her debut book.

She can be contacted at sur_2301@yahoo.co.uk